Writing to
DESCRIBE

Jill Jarnow

The Rosen Publishing Group's
PowerKids Press™
New York

Published in 2006 by The Rosen Publishing Group, Inc.
29 East 21st Street, New York, NY 10010

Copyright © 2006 by The Rosen Publishing Group, Inc.

All rights reserved. No part of this book may be reproduced in any form without permission in writing from the publisher, except by a reviewer.

First Edition

Editor: Frances E. Ruffin
Book Design: Emily Muschinske

Photo Credits: Cover (right) © LWA-Stephen Welstead/CORBIS; cover (left) © Jose Luis Pelaez, Inc./CORBIS; p. 15 © Joseph Muschinske.

Library of Congress Cataloging-in-Publication Data

Jarnow, Jill.
  Writing to describe / Jill Jarnow.— 1st ed.
    v. cm. — (Write now : a kid's guide to nonfiction writing)
  Includes bibliographical references and index.
  Contents: Writing to describe introduction — Choosing a topic — Making an outline — Using verbs to describe action — Using your five senses to describe — Making a poster — Writing a book report — What's fun about fun facts — Describing a journey — Describing with synonyms — Glossary.
  ISBN 978-1-4358-3802-4
  1. Report writing—Juvenile literature. 2. English language—Composition and exercises—Juvenile literature. 3. Description (Rhetoric)—Juvenile literature. [1. Report writing. 2. English language—Composition and exercises.] I. Title.

LB1047.3.J37 2005
372.62'3—dc22

2003024460

Manufactured in the United States of America

Contents

Writing to Describe	4
Choosing a Topic	6
Making an Outline	8
Using Verbs to Describe Action	10
Using Your Five Senses to Describe	12
Making a Poster	14
Writing a Book Report	16
What's Fun About Fun Facts	18
Describing a Journey	20
Describing with Synonyms	22
Glossary	23
Index	24
Web Sites	24

Writing to Describe

Students learn about a subject when they write a report. That's why teachers ask students to write book reports, social studies reports, and science reports. Think about it. To start a report, you gather facts and ideas by doing **research**. You have to understand a **topic** well enough to describe it in your own words.

There are two kinds of **descriptive** reports. General reports describe broad topics, such as bears or birds. **Specific** reports describe a certain kind of bear or bird, such as a grizzly bear or a sparrow. When you write to describe, you write **details** about people, places, or things.

A Descriptive Report Checklist

Be sure to include:

- ■ **A title**
- ■ **A topic sentence that tells what will be in the report**
- ■ **Details about the topic**
- ■ **Details that are arranged in an order that makes sense**
- ■ **A closing sentence that sums up the report**

Living Along the Shoreline — **Title**

Animals that live in the tidal zone have special features that help them to live. — **Topic sentence**

Some animals have thick, hard shells. Barnacles, which are saltwater animals with shells, stick to rocks along the shoreline. Clams have a little footlike part that helps them dig into the sand. Crabs use their claws and legs to dig into the sand and cover themselves. — **Details**

When the ocean's tides flow in and out, it affects animals in different ways. — **Closing sentence**

Choosing a Topic

To help choose an interesting topic, do research on a broad topic. You might want to write about **Pilgrims**. However, this is a large topic. To narrow the topic for your report, create an idea web. On a sheet of paper, draw a large circle for your main topic. Then add small circles to hold ideas about the main topic. For example, if the topic is "Pilgrims and food," your small circles might include the words "planting," "gathering," "hunting," "fishing," "cooking," and "sharing Thanksgiving dinner." These topics will help you to fill in the details, or facts that give more **information** on your topic.

A Descriptive Web

Creating a web will help you to organize your ideas on a topic. Planning the details you'd like to focus on will make for a more organized finished report.

- sharing Thanksgiving dinner
- planting
- gathering
- **The Pilgrims and Food**
- cooking
- fishing
- hunting

File This...

Before deciding on your topic, research the topic to make sure that there is enough information to write about.

1. Ask the librarian to show you where to find information about your topic.

2. Do your research quickly so you can get your first choice for a topic.

3. Keep notes so that you can find your research again easily.

Making an Outline

You may wonder how to start your descriptive report. Begin by making an outline. An outline is a plan of what will be in your report. From your research, choose the subjects you want to cover and the order in which they will appear.

Write the topic of your descriptive report at the top of a sheet of paper. Then list several main **headings**, or topics, about the subject. Below each main heading, list a **subhead**, or a fact about the topic, which provides your details. Put your topics and facts in order. The last main heading should describe how you will conclude, or end, your report.

An Outline

The First Thanksgiving — Topic and title

I. The Pilgrims — Use Roman numerals for your main heads

   A. The Pilgrims arrive on the *Mayflower*
   B. The Pilgrims settle in Plymouth
   C. The very cold winter of 1620

Use letters to list details in your subheads

II. Harvest Festivals

   A. Harvest celebrations in England
   B. Governor William Bradford announces a harvest festival
   C. Inviting the Native Americans

III. Preparing for the Feast

   A. Hunting and fishing
   B. Cooking the food

IV. Dinner is Served

   A. Native Americans arrive with gifts of food
   B. What food was served

V. Results of the Dinner — Closing topic

   A. Treaty signed between the Pilgrims and the Native Americans
   B. A national holiday

Using Verbs to Describe Action

> **Write Right!**
> Action verbs describe what someone or something does or has done.

Verbs are action words. They describe what is done. For example, "crawl," "walk," "sing," "dance," "talk," and "eat" are some action verbs that describe physical activities. Verbs can also describe quiet activities. "Think," "smell," and "love," are some quiet verbs. You may write in a first draft that your dog Duke "ate his dinner." To write a more interesting story, use lively verbs that describe how Duke "gulped" or "wolfed down" his dinner.

Finding the Action Verbs

The action verb in each sentence is colored red. For each sentence, think of some verbs that are more descriptive. Some possible answers are listed below.

1. My cousin talks on the phone.

2. The kite flew away.

3. John and Sue laugh at the jokes.

4. She ran upstairs.

5. He yelled at his little sister.

6. Bob will wash the dirt off his new shirt.

7. I like chocolate.

ANSWERS:
1. chats, whispers
2. sailed, floated
3. giggle, howl
4. darted, raced
5. screamed, boomed
6. brush, rub
7. crave, love

Using Your Five Senses to Describe

Do you remember a special meal that you shared with your family? Did you ever have a scary moment when you thought you were in danger? You can use your five senses to describe these events so that readers feel like they were there. To use your five senses in writing, choose words that describe what you saw, heard, smelled, tasted, and touched. If you must write a report about a class trip to the zoo, take along a pencil and paper. Make notes. Be aware of how your five senses are **affected** during your visit so that you can write a colorful, descriptive paper about your **experience** at the zoo.

A Report That Uses the Five Senses

A Cool Day at Wonderworld
by Jessica Larkin

When Christina and I went to Wonderworld, it was mobbed with people. The smell of popcorn and cotton candy filled the air. The salty popcorn made me thirsty. The flashing lights on the rides and games made us blink our eyes. We spent most of the day going on rides that made us dizzy. When we finally climbed into the Sky Flyer, the metal car was cold against my back and legs. The padded seat felt sticky. I thought the Sky Flyer was so cool. As the coaster climbed the tracks to the top, the only sound was the clicking of the wheels. Then the cars plunged down the tracks at about 100 miles per hour (161 km/h). I held on and screamed my head off! So did Christina. We loved the scary feeling, so we went on the Sky Flyer two more times!

The words in color are words that describe senses.

When you use your five senses to describe a trip to an amusement park or another favorite place, you can write a colorful report that is fun to read.

Making a Poster

Posters can be used to ask for help, to ask for information, or to announce an event. The most attention-getting posters use descriptive writing. For example, to make a poster that asks for help to find a lost dog, print "My Dog Is Lost" in large letters across the top of a sheet of paper. The poster can describe what the dog looks like and how it **behaves**. It will tell when and where the dog was lost, and how to **contact** you. If you are offering a **reward**, describe it at the bottom of your poster.

Write Right!

Write a telephone number on your poster telling the reader where you can be reached. Put a picture of your pet on the poster.

MY DOG IS LOST

My dog was lost on August 11, 2003, near 7th Avenue and Bergen Street. He has wavy brown and white fur. He's a springer spaniel and he has droopy eyes. He has an I.D. collar. He answers to the name Falf. He is very friendly. Leave messages for Dave at 555-1234 any time. There is a $100 reward.

Use a heading to catch the reader's attention.

A description will help people to recognize Falf if they see him.

Put Your Poster to Work

- Make photocopies of your poster.
- Hang your posters on community bulletin boards at school or the library.
- Ask store owners if you can hang posters in their windows or on bulletin boards in their stores.
- Be sure to remove your posters when you find your dog!

Writing a Book Report

Begin your book report with a description of the plot, or the main story. Write about the characters and the events, but do not give away the ending! If the book was **nonfiction**, describe the topic. Next write your **opinion** of the book. Describe what you enjoyed most. If you did not like the book, write your reasons. Was the main character hard to like? Did the story move too slowly? End your report by explaining what you think the author wanted to share with the readers.

> *Check It Out!*
>
> **Use adjectives to show that a book is funny, sad, or scary. An adjective is a word that describes a person, place, or thing.**

A Report About a Good Book

Dave at Night
by Gail Carson Levine
Book report by Marion Smith

The year is 1926. When Dave's father dies, Dave becomes an orphan. His relatives send him to live in a horrible orphanage for boys where the director hits the boys and steals from them. Dave plans to escape, but he can't until he gets back a carving that his father made, which the director stole. Dave sneaks out at night, but he always sneaks back in the morning. He meets many interesting characters and has many adventures.

There is a lot of sadness in this book, but it is also very funny. I couldn't stop reading it because I was anxious to know what would happen next. In Dave at Night, Gail Carson Levine describes how a brave person like Dave made bad things turn to good things. He kept trying to make things better for himself.

- Begin with a topic sentence.
- Use action verbs to make the story come to life.
- Write about what happened in the book.
- Tell the reader what you liked or did not like about the book.
- Close by describing the main idea.

What's Fun About Fun Facts

All descriptive reports include facts, which are pieces of information that are true and that can be proved. However, some writers use fun facts. These facts can be surprising, weird, scary, or hard to believe. Although they may be hard to believe, they are true. Fun facts add unusual descriptive information, and they can make the reader want to know more about a subject. Unusual facts can add fun to your report.

Check It Out!

Not every fact that is printed in a book or on the Internet is true. Check out all of your facts in books that you can trust, such as encyclopedias, atlases, and library books about the subject.

WEIRD-but-TRUE
Science Facts

These facts give important information, but in a fun way.

A daddy longlegs spider has legs that are from 5 to 20 times longer than its body. If this were the same for people, a person would have legs from 15 to 60 feet (4.5 to 18 m) long!

The ground cracked open in a Mexican cornfield near the village of Paricutin on February 20, 1943. A volcano was growing. On the first day the volcano grew to be 164 feet (50 m) tall. By 1952, nine years later, it had soared to more than 1,300 feet (396 m), and had buried two towns!

Most African elephants weigh less than a blue whale's tongue! In fact the blue whale's tongue is big enough for fifty full-grown people to stand on it!

Remember that fun facts are still facts. Do your research, and check your facts before adding them to your report.

The catfish has more than 27,000 taste buds in its mouth. This is more than any other animal in the world. In fact a catfish's whole body is covered in taste buds. A 6-inch (15-cm) catfish could have as many as 250,000 taste buds!

Describing a Journey

Have you ever taken a trip to another city, state, or country? Would you like to tell other people about your visit? Write a **travelogue**! A travelogue can be a talk or a piece of writing about travel. In a travelogue you can describe the people and places that you see on your **journey**.

Travelogues are often written in the style of a newspaper or magazine article. Travel writers may keep diaries while they travel. This way they can write descriptive short stories about the place they visited. They can describe the food they ate, the things they saw, and the adventures they had.

A Travelogue

Before your trip gather facts about the place you plan to visit from travel books and encyclopedias.

A Visit to Mexico
by Les Miller

If you are planning a trip to Mexico City, save a day to visit Teotihuac. It is near Mexico City. The buildings are made of brownish gray stone. In the past they were painted in bright colors. There are beautiful statues of ancient Mexican gods everywhere. Some were created to look like feathered snakes. The ancient people who lived at Teotihuac also built the Pyramid of the Sun and the Pyramid of the Moon. The pyramids are buildings shaped like triangles. The Pyramid of the Sun is about 200 feet (61 m) high. The weather was blazing hot. We stopped and had lunch in a restaurant that was in a cave. More than 800 people could eat there. The cave was cool inside. We ate a delicious chicken dish with rice. As I rode back to Mexico City, I thought that Teotihuac seemed like a place on another planet.

Use descriptive words so that your readers feel that they are there.

Describing with Synonyms

Do you tend to describe things with the same words over and over again? Using the right words can make your writing more exciting. Synonyms can make your writing clearer and stronger. A synonym is a word that has the same meaning, or almost the same meaning, as another word. For example, the words "start" and "begin" are synonyms. Other synonyms can mean somewhat different things, like "sleep," "nap," and "snooze." All good writers use a dictionary to find definitions and a **thesaurus** to find synonyms. Also, good writers know that descriptive words are fun to read and fun to write.

Glossary

affected (uh-FEKT-ed) Changed.
behaves (bih-HAYVZ) Acts.
contact (KON-takt) To get in touch with someone.
descriptive (dih-SKRIP-tiv) Using words to give a picture.
details (DEE-taylz) Extra facts.
experience (ik-SPEER-ee-ents) Knowledge or skill gained by doing or seeing something.
headings (HED-ingz) Titles for pages or chapters.
information (in-fer-MAY-shun) Knowledge or facts.
journey (JER-nee) Traveling from one place to another.
nonfiction (non-FIK-shun) Writing that is about real life.
opinion (uh-PIN-yun) A belief that is based on what a person thinks rather than what is known to be true.
Pilgrims (PIL-grimz) The people who sailed on the *Mayflower* in 1620 from England to America in search of freedom to practice their beliefs.
research (REE-serch) Careful study.
reward (rih-WARD) A prize.
specific (spih-SIH-fik) Stated in a way that is clear and easily understood.
subhead (SUB-hed) A less important heading or title.
thesaurus (thih-SOR-us) A book or list of words that are alike and words that are different from each other.
topic (TAH-pik) The subject of a piece of writing.
travelogue (TRA-veh-log) A talk or a piece of writing about travel.

Index

D
details, 4, 6, 8
draft, 10

F
five senses, 12
fun facts, 18

H
heading(s), 8

I
idea web, 6
information, 6, 14, 18

N
nonfiction, 16

O
outline, 8

P
posters, 14

R
report, 4, 6, 8, 12, 16
research, 4, 6, 8

S
subhead, 8
synonyms, 22

T
topic(s), 4, 6, 8, 16
travelogue, 20

V
verbs, 10

Web Sites

Due to the changing nature of Internet links, PowerKids Press has developed an online list of Web sites related to the subject of this book. This site is updated regularly. Please use this link to access the list:
www.powerkidslinks.com/wnkw/writdes/

www.ingramcontent.com/pod-product-compliance
Lightning Source LLC
LaVergne TN
LVHW071654060526
838200LV00029B/452